The Quest of the Fairies

Trish Champion

Balboa Press books may be ordered through booksellers or by contacting:

Balboa Press
A Division of Hay House
1663 Liberty Drive
Bloomington, IN 47403
www.balboapress.com
1 (877) 407-4847

ISBN: 978-1-9822-1923-9 (sc)
978-1-9822-1924-6 (e)

Library of Congress Control Number: 2018915256

Print information available on the last page.

Balboa Press rev. date: 01/09/2019

BALBOA.
PRESS
A DIVISION OF HAY HOUSE

It would soon be time for the Moon Dance Festival. All of Kaylee's friends, the wood sprites, the elves and the gnomes would be there. Kaylee's best friend Julyn would be there too.

Kaylee and Julyn were fairies. They lived in the most enchanted, beautiful realm called Forest-in-the-Valley, in the land of Lumuria. Everyone called it "Mu" for short.

Kaylee and Julyn were busy picking the colorful windflowers that grew everywhere in the Valley. They would have just enough time to weave them into a splendid crown of fragrant colors for their lavender hair. They would finish off the crowns of brilliant color by tying long strands of ribbon to flow with their long manes of hair.

Everyone was gathering now down in the glen. There was a hurried, hushed air about all of the enchanted creatures of Mu. Kaylee and Julyn were no exception. Their golden-tipped wings got them there just in time for the magical orb of crimson and golden fireflies to descend toward everyone.

As the orb of fireflies touched the ground, it became ablaze with light as if indeed there was a real fire. At that moment, all of the fairies, gnomes, elves, and wood sprites began a wondrous dance of joy as the moon above cast its silvery light through the evergreen branches.

Suddenly, from the center of the glowing crimson light of the fireflies the Queen of Lumuria appeared. Everyone became quite still, for they knew her unexpected appearance meant that she had something of great importance to tell them. It was difficult to look right at her, for she illuminated such a beautiful whitish, golden glow that it took a few moments for everyone's eyes to adjust.

As she opened her arms and lifted her head, she sparkled like a million tiny stars and said, "I am glad to be here on this festive occasion of the Moon Dance. However, I must tell you of something that is troubling me. As you know, we exist because of our belief in love and harmony. Recently I was in the Chamber of Light and noticed one of the spheres of light was growing dim. In time, I'm afraid it will be gone forever." With this, everyone gasped disbelievingly.

Kaylee looked at Julyn who had big tears forming in her eyes. "How can this be?" Julyn pleaded to Kaylee. The queen continued, "We do have one ray of hope. There is a place called Mystic Mountain. In this most enchanted place, there lives a wise Wizard. He is the only one who can help us. I am afraid I need to ask who among you could journey there to speak to him of our most desperate need."

Kaylee and Julyn held each other tight. They could not believe what they had just heard. Then in the same instant, they looked into each other's eyes. They knew what they must do.

The next day they met with the queen in the Chamber of Light. It felt so good to be there. The light and love that radiated from this place and from each of the beings in their world was truly wonderful. True to what the queen had said, one of the spheres of light was indeed growing dim. The queen looked kindly at each of them and said, "I must tell you how happy it makes me feel to know the people of my realm want to help. I am pleased that you both have come forward. For it is you Kaylee, and you Julyn, who I believe can succeed in this quest."

Lumuria was a vast and beautiful land. With its green valleys, snow covered mountains, crystal clear streams and rivers, Kaylee and Julyn knew most of their travels would be pleasant. Nevertheless, in the back of their minds was the knowledge that there was something wrong. The queen had tried to explain it to them, but could not make clear exactly what was wrong or how to change it.

Flying just above the tall, dewy grass and blossoms of dazzling color in one of the many meadows, they looked up and saw before them the grandest mountain they had ever seen. They could barely see the peak, for it was shrouded in a mysterious cloud of purple and coral haze. They knew this must be Mystic Mountain.

It was at this moment that Kaylee suggested they stop for a little rest. Julyn was glad and at the same time relieved, asking, "What do you think the Wizard will be like?" Kaylee studied the scene before them and replied, "It has to be a fantastic place. Anyone with that kind of wisdom must be the most amazing person, being, creature or whatever he is!"

They were just about to leave when they heard a small, sort of raspy voice croak, "Hey! Who are you and what are you doing in this meadow? I haven't seen fairies around here since, since I can't remember when!"

Kaylee and Julyn looked up to see a curious little fellow dressed in what appeared to be large flower buds. On his head of curly red hair, he wore a laurel of holly. His scent reached the two fairies before he did.

"Did you hear what I asked?" bellowed the colorful fellow.

After blinking hard several times, Julyn was the first to say, "Wwwho are you?"

"Why I'm Lesscot, apprentice to his royal mightiness, the Wizard of Mystic Mountain! We hardly ever see anyone around here anymore. It seems as if the creatures of the land of Mu don't need us!"

"Well indeed we do! That is why we are here. We need to seek the wisdom of the Wizard in hopes that he can help our people in the Forest-in-the-Valley," blurted Kaylee forgetful that she had never seen a whatever-he-was. With that, the two fairies explained their problem of the sphere of light growing dim.

Hearing this, Lesscot stood up and exclaimed, "So this is what my master has been trying to explain to me for so long and now I understand! Follow me!"

"Wait just a minute!" insisted Julyn. "We know who you are, but we've never seen anyone like you."

Looking thoughtful for a moment, his hoarse voice explained, "I guess you could call me a flower sprite. After becoming interested in changing and growing into something that had more meaning for me, I came to the Wizard. That's when I started to transform from a wood sprite into what you see before you now."

Satisfied, Kaylee and Julyn followed Lesscot toward the mountain. Despite its lush and fragrant paths that led up the steep slopes, the fairies kept a safe distance behind Lesscot. Unexpectedly, he disappeared. Starring in the direction he vanished from, they stopped, unsure if they should go on. As unexpectedly as he disappeared, he reappeared.

"Come on. What are you waiting for?"

"Where did you go?" they asked.

Lesscot explained, "There are many entrances to the inner chambers of this mountain. All appear to be hidden to the untrained eye. Just stay with me and all will be made clear."

As the three of them entered the cavern, a soothing sound of the most unusual, beautiful music filled their heads. At the same time, a warmth they had not known since times past surrounded them. "Come, my master appears to be expecting you."

After some time and what seemed to be a maze of never-ending turns, they suddenly came into a huge room. It had a cathedral ceiling and seemed to be made of crystal – for the most warm, glowing light poured into the room from all directions. It made the room appear to be sparkling with jeweled light. The music continued to fill their heads 'til they felt almost dizzy. Kaylee and Julyn could not tell where it was coming from. It did not matter. They felt as though they could have stayed there forever!

Then, in the front of the cavern, a ball of glistening light took form in the shape of the Wizard. His robes gleamed with a sparkling rosy, golden color. His face and hair seemed to be of the same colors, with only his eyes illuminating the coolest shade of emerald green.

"Come here to me my little ones," his gentle voice beckoned. "Tell me why you have come."

Kaylee and Julyn relayed the entire story of their queen's concern for the sphere of light – the symbol of their people's being – wondering why it was growing dimmer by the hour, and how she needed volunteers to seek the Wizard's help.

Looking quite serene he said, "Sometimes what appears to be a problem that has no visible answer is when we should look inside ourselves to listen for the truth. I believe that once Fear rears its ugly head, we start to believe in it instead of our own inner truth. That truth being that in every one of us is the power to create our own destinies and peace. The reason the sphere of light is growing dim is because your people are starting to doubt their inner beauty and strength and believe in the monster called Fear. Once all of you reclaim your inner strength by believing in yourselves, the sphere of light will once again shine brightly."

Stunned that the answer seemed so simple, Kaylee and Julyn embraced each other. Tears of joy streamed down their cheeks. They looked to thank the great Wizard, but he was gone. They would remember forever his magical presence, his emerald eyes and his gentle voice, and most of all his message of Truth.

Turning to go, the fairies found themselves standing once again outside the hidden entrance with Lesscot. As they looked at him, they noticed his face was aglow with happiness. His flower buds were now in full bloom, and along with a noticeably smoother voice he exclaimed, "Thank you, Kaylee and Julyn! You've helped me too!"

"Without you, we're sure our quest would have been very difficult indeed. You came just when we needed you. I guess deep inside we must have believed in ourselves all along. We just needed to be reminded of our inner strength."

With this knowledge, the fairies raced home and shared what they had learned with their people. They told of meeting Lesscot and their journey into Mystic Mountain. They told of the wondrous sights and sounds they had experienced. They also told of the evil monster, Fear, and how it can destroy them and their way of life, if they chose to believe in it instead of their inner light and beauty.

Then, as all of the gnomes, elves, wood sprites and fairies finished listening to Kaylee's and Julyn's story, the Queen of Lumuria appeared. Smiling lovingly, she told them how grateful she was for their safe return from their quest. Above all, she was hopeful the Wizard's message would help to remind the people of their realm the truth of their being – and – to the cheers of all gathered, announced that the sphere of light had begun to shine brighter than ever before!

Trish Champion (known to her students as Dr. C) is a lifetime educator whose passion in life is to excite and instill in young, active minds the idea of pursuing knowledge, being curious and seeking adventure. Many years ago, she created *The Quest of the Fairies* for her young daughter who was having trouble falling asleep, which in turn gave life to the wondrous land of Mu and the beings who live there. This story, in a way, reflects Dr. C's life – one filled with her own never ending quest; searching for knowledge, enlightenment – and believing in oneself. Dr. C has spent more than 30 years in education, which includes teaching various grade levels, gifted & talented, and higher education, where she currently teaches for the University of Iowa. She sincerely hopes you enjoy *The Quest of the Fairies*!

Printed in the United States
By Bookmasters